Kiki

Kiki

AMANDA
EARL

CHAUDIERE BOOKS MMXIV

Dire que l'entreprise est simple ou sans danger serait fou. Déranger les anges!
Jean Cocteau,"Par lui-même", *1927 Vocabulaire Plain-Chant*

Books must have fire and shadow.
Jean Cocteau, *Opium, the Diary of a Cure*

Contents

Preface

Costume parties where Kisling dressed up as the madame of a Marseilles brothel, night clubs named after operas, painters living together in a beehive, poets and artists duelling, artists painting false eyes on actors and actresses for a film, late night private clubs, opium dens ... this was Montparnasse between the wars.

Apollinaire, Picasso, Modigliani, Matisse, Foujita, Hemingway, Fitzgerald and others came together to gossip and argue, to discuss their work, to drink until dawn and to celebrate life after the horrors of World War I, with a depression looming and another war about to begin.

One of the most exuberant celebrants was Alice Ernestine Prin, who came to Paris at thirteen to live with her mother and ended up becoming Kiki, the Queen of Montparnasse. She danced and sang in cabarets, flaunted her sexuality, she painted, she got arrested in Nice, she starred in avant-garde silent films, she went to the United States to try out for Paramount and came back because she didn't have her comb, she modelled for Man Ray, Gargallo, Foujita, Kisling, Alexander Calder, and others. Kiki was everywhere.

The era and place she called home housed some of the most playful and innovative works of art, literature, theatre and music history has ever seen. The book pays homage to les années folles, the crazy years, to Kiki, her friends, and her lovers and those creative spirits who came after.

ALICE

This is Alice. This is fucked up. These are the mushrooms, the fraises de terre and dandelions we salvaged from acid soil. Maman's bastard children always hungry, our dirty nails clawing the ground.

This is the limestone that resists our frail bodies.

We gulp down the mushrooms washed in the Source de la Doix. Trumpet shaped egg yellow, dark brown and honey combed. Cream stemmed dreams or instant death. We eat. We live. This is not a choice.

This is Alice. This is fucked up. I pluck black currant leaves for my godfather's moonshine cassis. My reward is a small sip of eau-de-vie. My fingers are purple and sweet. The nape of my neck is scorched and sore. My back aches from stooping so low. My body shivers with the heat of all this.

This is Alice. This is fucked up. This is opium. This is the drug I share with Cocteau, his gold brocade jacket in Achille S's back room, blinding. We paint; we compose an opera and I am Kiki. I wear pearls. I drink red wine and sing love songs to old reprobates in the boîtes. Kiki in a box.

I am Kiki with bread and onion in the pocket of my threadbare coat. Red wine keeps me warm on the sacs at the Gare du Montparnasse.

I strip for five francs in Soutine's studio. I steal his bread and wine. I am naked. I am thirteen. I bruise my lips a bitten apple red, strawberry red. I darken my brows with matchsticks and I burn.

I am quick silvered glass, made of mercury.
I can throw you off balance in the swing of a mood.

Man Ray oh Man Ray of light. Yankie mama's boy with pidgin French like a toddler learning his ABCs. Satie, Foujita, like them. I think of the possibilities for good meals. A good strong vin de table. Man gives me a hat to make me his lady and later his bedroom gutter slut. I sing when he plays me. He inks cello markings into my back, brands me, but the ink runs, stains his lily white tapis. His hands. I can feel them now, stroking. I am untameable. My chum, my petite amie, Mady, the panther. We slink along in the night and roar on rooftops. Hemingway should set us up in Africa, abandon the little woman and Bumby.

I'm looking at my grave. The rotting flowers on my grave. Why does no one tend my grave? Like Miss Diamonds crumbling into paste, I am vermin and compost, the stench of raw onions planted in the dirt.

I take food to Lucy. Pauvre Lucy, mon amie. Pascin and his bombes, the final one, not a party, but his wrists cut, he made his adieu to his love, a message in blood on the mirror. In my reflection I see his ghost. I can no longer walk past mirrors.

I carry a slice of obsidian wrapped in cloth. I cup my face tightly in my hands.

I am transfixed. I yield to the rock's sharp edge.

When the blood has soaked my reflection, I let go.

This is Alice. This is fucked up. Man Ray paints my face as if I am his canvas. Each day a different eyebrow shade. I am his made up doll, his ticket to Montparnasse. He is Kiki's man.

.

Not far from my flat on the rue Bréa, street carnivals and gypsy fortunes. For ten sous, the tower falls over and over. I could have had a bowl of soup at Rosalies. She wouldn't give me bread. I had crumbs in my pockets.

I love strawberries. They are like sex. Better than. I get them in bins at the Café Select or le Jockey. Ripe and plump red windfall from gâteaux, sweet icing clinging to the berry. I lick it off. I love to lick.

I am Nero's emerald, the decoration of an emperor gone mad.
Hard. Precise. Sharp. Rare.
I fiddle while Man Ray burns.

These are the men between the wars that come to Paris and expect to find ... what? Life? This is too big a word. I sit in their laps and they feed me, give me pearls. Shiny pure white pearls. I devour these men and their brilliance. White pearls. An Egyptian black cat. Stroke me. In these arms, salvation. I'll rock you to sleep, bébé. Maman will cradle you.

I tell all the boys: Tzara, Soupault, Aragon, Breton. They're nattering again to Man.

Man puts me in another box, a silent box. I am pale. I am black and white. I am absolute. I am a mechanical contraption, all dancer. A star.

In the theatre I am monstrous, giant, a monster's face and thin eyebrows. The artificial bow of my tongue tied mouth. I could devour this city.

I could swallow the lights and be brilliant. I travel by ship to New York City. All this brilliance needs a tower. An empire state.

I am small in the new world. I am Alice again down the hole.

I shrink. I cannot eat what says eat me. I can only drink until I am Kiki again. Until I am back through the shattered glass.

My distortion is concave in the yellow amulet.
The gleam in the eye of an Egyptian cat.
A glass of Pernod, cloudy after a drop of water is added.

This is Alice. This is the night. This is fucked up. Street lamps in front of le Jockey still burning. Men at public urinals, street repair workers' sparks in the dark. Miss Diamonds has fallen asleep, gossiping about Pablo Picasso and Gertrude Stein. I am alone, the table rocks on uneven legs. Absinthe spills from a fallen glass, sugar thick in the bottom. This morning I'll have wormwood dreams.

This is Alice. This is fucked up. I sell garlic and shallots in the rue Mouffetard. I oil my curls, put gypsy combs in my hair and I am Kiki. I sing. I sell more garlic. I tighten my corset with string. Maman stuffs cotton down my front to give me big boobs. I wonder if this will lead to more bread, more wine. I rouge my lips with her fake flowers, yank the petals off one by one, wiping the dust away to uncover the red.

I sift in the big closet and turn white. I am a flour ghost. The old baker strips to his birthday suit, tells his dirty jokes in the nude to make me blush, but I don't. I turn the iron bar until the flour is smooth enough for bread. I choose the softest baguettes and hoard them in my pockets.

This is Alice. This is fucked up. A geezer sits on a bench near the Tuileries. I choose him to pluck me. The way he strums his guitar. He takes me to his small room at the top of a winding flight of stairs. He sings to me about the moon. I wear his nightgown. We lie down together. Sleep. In the morning all my petals intact.

My chum beds an old Corsican. He feeds her cheese and sausages. I watch them make love and feast on the unguarded sausage.

I am mica on the porticos of Rome.
I can see my every move.
When I dance, I can see myself shimmer.
After the patina flakes off, I am naked and bronze, shivering
in a puddle of gold.

This is Alice. This is fucked up. Cowboys and Indians square off on the walls of le Jockey. Men with wild west dreams spoil for a brawl. The tables are nailed down. Dark suits rub against dancehall floozies while I belt out "Les Filles de Camaret se disent toutes vierges." Pimps and goons hunch over banquettes, chatting up wallflowers, their future whores. I pass hookers on cobblestones beneath streetlamps. In Man's bed he wants to know why I'm always so hungry.

I am a Medici cabinet of mirrors.
There is me and me and me and me.
Kiki mocks me many times with her upturned nose.

I walk beneath the bridges at the Quai des Orfèvres. It's cold. Light snow falling on the Seine. I drop centimes on stacked up crates. They glisten beneath the moon. I leave behind the heel of a stale baguette, the dregs of my red wine in a green bottle. A hand emerges from a pile of rags.

These are the gargoyles that guard Paris and I am Esmeralda, entertaining all the quasimodos, straightening their lumps with torch songs, anthems and troubadour ballads. Their bells ring long after I'm gone.

I am Kiki, named by Fojita? I can't remember now, for my hairless twat. Men line up to see me, hear me sing. So what? Thérèse Treize tarts me up, dresses me in flowing skirts I raise between chansons to give the fellas a peek. They buy me glass after glass of red wine. I down each one d'un trait, in one gulp. Belt out my sauciest numbers, my lips stained with cheap burgundy.

I am silver.
Cool and sharp as a knife.

I am a siren garnished with rubies and diamonds.
Don't assume all I do is glitter.

This is Alice. This is fucked up. I'm a bird with pointed nose.
I am a crow. Back to Châtillon-sur-Seine, to Grandmaman
and the forest. I eat another mushroom. I am Alice. I am
down the hole again. I sit in the shade of green underbrush,
my knees scratched by low lying bushes, by strawberries. I
pop one in my mouth. My face and fingers are sticky with
juice.

I am a bodiless head sculpted in metal by Pablo Gargallo. He
art decoes me and cubes me. Tells me stories of le Bateau-
Lavoir, of Picasso and the dog, Frika.

I am a window made of paper,
a fragile silhouette that goes up in flames
with the merest touch of light.

We wander past the beehive, Eiffel's old Ruche where Modigliani and his pals shacked up when they were skint like me. I buzz around and hope for honey.

I am a tangle of electrical wire, shaped by Sandy Calder at 7, rue Cels, another one of the Yank's circus acts for the newsreels. I want cranks and pulleys to set me in perpetual motion.

This is Alice. This is fucked up. These are the ghosts of the Bal Mabille and la Grande Chaumière at Boulevard du Montparnasse and Boulevard d'Enfer. Céleste Mogador, Louise Voyageur, Rigolboche, Marie L'Absinthe dancing under acacia trees. Dancing for pleasure. Dancing for business. Dancing for the mania of touch. The polka, the waltz and the cancan, the chatter of courtisanes in the long post revolutionary nights. I am Kiki and I toss and turn in the rumpled sheet, yanked out of my dreams, my sleepless eyes bruised by late blue afternoons.

This is Alice. This is fucked up. I am the thorns stripped bare of roses. I am Queen of Montparnasse. The petals float back to the Source de la Douix, to Marie Esprit, to the shepherds. Back to Marie Ernestine Prin at Châtillon, rose arranged in metal type as eros.

I wear a mirror dress to lure all of you even the saints.
I am an ounce of arsenic, poisonous but useful.

I am a half ounce of charred wine sediment.
You can't resist drinking me down to the dregs.

I am a jet black pocket mirror in an ivory box.
Black hair, white powdered face of a geisha.

This is Alice. This is fucked up. I had to bash the cop, didn't I? He tried to grope my tits, so I went for him. I'd do it again. I'm no floozy butterfly flitting around the sailors. Man Ray, my Yank in shining armour, says I'm high strung. I'll give them all high strung.

The Villefranche jail almost did me in. I swallowed my words to get back to Man and the costume balls at Parnasse. I'll sing and dance and drink and forget this dark cell, these Niçois salauds.

This is Alice. This is fucked up. This is Berlin. This is the Bal Musette. This is cocaine and I am shit-faced. Fünf minuten, fünf minuten, in five minutes I have to belt 'em out, swivel my hips on stage and sing for these square-heads. Oh Maman, they pay me good dough. Soon I'll be home. I'll take care of you. I promise. Je te jure.

This is Alice. This is fucked up. The krauts have invaded Paris. Floozies drape their bodies over the brown uniforms. Hitler tours la Closerie des Lilas. Man Ray is gone. Soutine is gone. Picasso is gone, but I remain to wander the cobblestones and drink another glass.

This is Alice. This is fucked up. I doll myself up for another night Chez Kiki. In the mirror, I see my fifty two years, the Burgundy sky, strawberries, the sacs at the Gare du Montparnassse, nights filled with song and red wine or spent in Man Ray's bed. The reflection of an open window.

I am tethered by ribbon and iron hooks.
The men of Montparnasse. A not so tender trap?

I am common glass.
I am the broken fragments.
I am ugly, a nightmare kaleidoscope.
I am mad. I am naked. I don't know what I am.

TALES OF MONTPARNASSE

Crack goes the peel of innocence,
says Harriet Monroe.

Cats talk to buttered Picassos
in classic Brancusi hats.

Ziegfeld is desolate
as a tumbler.

Titus edits paper angels
at the Café Select.

Gaudier-Brzeska's eggplants
shave cowboys at the
Closerie des Lilas.

Harpence's salon is festooned
with lines of caraway.

Jeanne H's anatomy
ornaments the art of letters.

Mr. Peggotty smears
dancing silk plants
with strawberry ovum.

Mais oui, Mina
would trouble Eliot's
box of renaissance.

The destiny of Marcel
du Champ is a musical onion.

Kandinsky milks writers
who love ornaments
in European poses.

Burgundy's gunsmith girls
design battle scenes in mirrors.

Dumas and de Plumas complicate
corpses on the rue Mouffetard.

Inner Miss Toklas
is carried away by Aragon
and Breton on the same
surrealist ship.

Inner drinks
with Gertrude Stein.

Kean petals money
from Miss Diamonds' abstract box.

Wives hunt
by the door for winter
and Eliot.

Eastman veals guitars
on the rue Vavin.

Zadkine drinks filtré
and smokes Gauloises,
forming handkerchiefs
of clouds at the Café Select.

Anne Boelyn's ovum pearls
in the faces of European Dadaists.

Youki's a woman of glass
dandelions from a
Saint-Vorles studio.

Smoke to define blood
on Tristan Tzara's quilt.

Greedy corpses subscribe
to the Blue Sultan.

Wyndham's house
is heavily magazined
with the people of Valencia.

Stieglitz hears illusions
on a ship of maquillage.

Champagne Dadaists pout
for Tristan Tzara and Philippe Soupault.

The Great Gatsby
tames cool bones
cracking to hurry.

The Saturday Evening Post
is serious as a death-mask.

Kisling and O'Keefe
rise like angels with horses.

Marcel du Champ and
Marcel du Champ mirror
faces with blackbirds.

Pre-war Dumas
cavorts with women
as limey as oxydized lamps.

Blood-stained snow
leads to icy novels
by Stieglitz.

Freemasons sketch Stravinsky's
mouth and heart.

Hennaed Leo S.
is greedy at the joy tabac.

Unknown women and Max arrive
with appetites like William
from a tasselled silent film.

Grenadines in diabolos
shout euphemisms at
bracelet lesbians in the
Gyspy Bar.

Dandelions hallucinate the peal
of ghosts in the Bastille.

Green-covered spectors
mask hard-boiled eggs in
la Galerie des Monstres.

Daphne and Yvette wear arsenic hats
at the sign of the Black Manikin.

Lily Kandinsky creates a sacred
animation of peep-holes.

Studio foreheads flog boy oil
at le Jockey on Saint-Vorles.

Coloured jewels talk to St. Bernard
de Clarivaux's hat for money
and poppy tea in le Jockey.

Rupert hands sleep
to expatriates lounging in hip
studios while supping on
gâteaux mocha and muguet truths.

the Tien Shan woman
tests her ripe red repertoire
on the rue Vavin.

Blackbirds firework
la Horde du Montparnasse.

Fresh from the cat, snow stains
blood paganism in leather.

Zadkine's Marguerita paints blackbirds.

Drunk Foujita inspires cures
for modesty.

Lipschitz' gypsy combs
are sweet as blackbirds.

Frizzy femmes damnées
shiver with Schwitters.

Yvette G's telephone
is green as a silent film.

de Clarivaux's shadow
empties into a gallery
of straw and pine.

The Toothless Measuring Worm
is in the courtyard
with Harriet Monroe.

Editors walk handbells to Marguerita,
la Dame aux Camellias.

Saturday Evening Posts gambol
in low-heeled affectation
at the pine woods of wealthy dreams.

Gather cocaine
for the Delmas captives,
the hair leathered corpses
chez le Dôme.

Man Ray frosts the shadows
along the Châtillon-sur-Seine.

Éluard animates
Paramount rhinestones.

Petals pine for their mamans
on the rue Vavin.

Modigliani's hair
streams from the design
of gunsmiths.

Breton's teeth are windows
wide for cocaine in the
Source de la Douix.

Segovia enflames the grease
of troubled editors.

In pajamas, Segovia
discusses apples
with Brassaï.

A raging gourmand phones
the elusive Daphne B.,
a scoundrel lonely for fistfights.

Soupault and Tzara
pout for Dadaist champagne.

Grandmaman's cliffhanger breasts
are languorous as Ariadne and Salomé.

Mady Lequeux dies of garlic
at Rosalies in the winter
of an abstract gallery.

Blackbirds and arsenic ciphers
are fireworked.

Maman pines for petals
in her glass of fire
at la Bastille.

O
P
I
U
M

"Opium : speed in silk"

This is opium heated on steel.
This is a lamp filled with perfumed oil.
This is a pipe covered with ivory and mother of pearl.

I am silvered.
I am thick as paste.
I am the dross.
I am the raw pill.
I am the alkaloid, the exquisite poison.
I close my eyes.
I count the white poppy tears falling like rain from Burgundy skies.

I am Helen of Troy, mixing elixirs. I am nepenthe.
I am a sunless sea and a lifeless ocean. This is alchemy.

I am the cherry, the fig tree, the luminous escape
from a metal box.

I am a master dot, a formless fugitive, a piece of marble.

I am the charmed lizard above the lamp. I am a season. I am the abandoned ghost.
The poppy is a blessing.

I am the rhythm of flowers, the speed of metal. I am a slow rising balloon.

I am a shadow cut out of paper.
I am dark as an enigma. I am a red poppy.
I am a matte vase that swallows light.
I remove my mask.
I lie prone on the ground,
a flower's stem impaled in my chest.
Red the only colour.
Breadfruit, cerise, feverroot, calambour,
grenadine, amaranth on my tongue.
I am wrapped in uncut velvet, crepe rubber,
tofu suede, ooze leather, butea frondosa
and glutinous honeycomb.

I am Euridice. I have fallen. I am dead.
I am a mirror.
I don the gloves. I swim.
I push against my miserable reflection.
The mirror ripples. A bell rings.
I am made of mirrors reflecting the sun.
I am Pandora. Open the box.

I am a wound, a face painted on the window.
I am a burn mark on the back of the neck.
I am a five pointed star inked on the skin.
I am a tangled knot of string hanging from the ceiling.
I plunge my hands into the bowl.
My hand is a wound. My hand is a drowned
mouth spewing water, demanding air.
I am the morning. I am the crowing rooster.
I am the awakened statue.
I press my hand against the mirrored glass.
I jump through the mirror.
I am a tiny swimmer in the dark. I fade. I reappear.
I raise my arms.
I am a hotel.
I am the worn out leather shoes by the door.
I am a keyhole. I am door #17.
I am on the boulevard Arago in Mexico.
I am shot. I fall to the ground.
I am shadows on the ceiling of room #18.
I am a young girl covered with bells.
I am a severe witch dressed in black.
I am flogged. I climb the walls and the ceiling,
bells still ringing.
I am a desperate hermaphrodite in room #23.
I am death surrounded by stars.
I drag myself back through the mirror.
I pulverize the statue.
I throw a snowball and murder a child.

I am the knocked down child.
I am the blood bubbling from the lips of the child.
I am glory. I am destiny. I am playing cards.
I am the child's corpse at the feet of the players.
I am the ace of hearts. I am lost.
I am the audience. I am an eye patch, diamonds and a white feathered fan.
I am an onlooker. I remove my mask.
I am the guardian angel with wings and an insect body on my back.
I pull the ace of hearts from the corpse's jacket pocket.
I am shiny and black.
I cover the body with my own.
I take the ace of hearts away.
I am the pistol from the pocket of the card player.
I am the trigger.
I am the dead man. I am the blood that falls on the ground beside the
King of Hearts.
I am the woman with the long black gloves. My eyes are dark.
I am the statue. I am the ox with harp and globe.
I am a smokestack. I am demolition. I collapse into rubble.

If a storm comes, Paris, the beautiful voyeur, will rub itself all over me.

I have written my name on a tree. Trees are better than marble because you can see your name grow.

When the earth is part sun and part shadow, it is a jungle panther. My friend, you have blood on your beak.

I have thrown my blue ink over tricks of death and turned sudden ghosts into blue trees. I have disturbed the angels.

IN WHICH K MEETS B IN A DREAM

"The Word is divided into units which be all in one piece and should be so taken, but the pieces can be had in any order being tied up back and forth in and out fore and aft like an innaresting sex arrangement."

William S. Burroughs, *Naked Lunch*, Atrophied Preface

They discuss tea heads, opium eaters. K. smokes from a long jade handle. B. sticks pins into his thighs, lets the heroin dribble in.

It's ugly, she tells him, your time is ugly.

I'm not the one with no gotch, pissing in the street, he says. How much green goop can you drink til you're psychedelic?

How many holes in your body till you're a wind instrument?

Metal with tourists, dear reader.

Rubbish, says B, it's unsteady, a distant shore.
Wet arrowheads volleying down, lady.

Green and delicate in the dawn.

Meatballs, baby, a train of salt from the east passing ass, it bangs and snarls,
says the pitchman. Vikings dissolve crackled prophesies through
antennae, yell into crystal for a rush.

A revelation of sniffled grey ooze
in cocaine innocence.

That's a heap, a spadeful with legs flat as a non-payment.

Here is a gift of dirty murders in pieces peeled in absence from virtual habits. If you have the guts to suck the threads up, bushmaster.

A body of transmutations, whinnies titillations vicariously between your thighs. Leaps onto your toes, fingers your codices in heat.

Get the message? Trees toddle here, sheriff. Behinds are phosphorescent as nutmeg. Deep cheeked mutterings of boys please radios.

Corn fish, lady.

Pick up the pinpoint of the orgasm, sister, citizen.

Second hand acts are sacrosanct as prairie streets, hustler.

It's an overcoat of rose deaths thawing at the kick of mischance, mandrake.

Naked, the last blind blackboard seller in bed.

Disconnect. Infected. Picture this. Skid row veins. A riot of workers dropping live iron claws.

Snakes in kaleidoscope vistas. Years in the pathos subway.

Pain artists floating farts in a medley of flash and dub for the criminally blonde.

A noise injected slam of tunes and tongues.

Your directions yodel like a rasp, snapping and growling, drifter.

This is water goof-balled,
an inscrutable hind leopard
shoving branches into pathic closets
to scream for sex, you occluder.

Sherry mouths caterwauling rolls, old time lemur.

You yellow out of focus ass blower.

Schmeck this. Cairo winds spill snapping trances to shutter fuck affection.

This disgraces phantom
pages in pathos twilight, man.

It's smoke off powder cells.
Users unlock hearts outraging the absently sick.

It is lost and trailing reflections. You are juiced. Amputate this river,
sad-eyed asp.

The putt putt fan of Ramadan's ectoplasm.
Nature on the brain trains huge flutes of tobacco, are you aware?

In order of long hard-ons.
Hoard this jungle chair tied down
by the land of word.

Sincere rabies are archetypical of balls, sailor.

It's prophetic. A sea of necks bleeding. Lush killed tea-rooms screaming hungry in the berserk aisle.

A displaced connotation whistling underwater taxis out of thirsty pants.

Pluck this. Return.
Rape transmissions, hat wearer.

You are complicit,
a cure for crabs. Oval masturbation.

You hold the flesh and rotten hourglass, sir.
I am quick as Texas in your hand. I warn you, bullhead.
God's junkies slam steel afterbirths, watcher.
You've got a withered sigh in your shot glass.
We flame in coils of spirit lamps as a gesture of burning delight.
Junk comes from culture to cop goofs and rancid quitters, scrap shifter.
This is a death pushing site where you wake, boy.
A mighty event of unfolding claws, reporter.

It's cerebral as horse,
raw as Ouab. Hungry as terror.
A throbbing hero fossil scrolling
up morphine peddled screams, cornhole.

No, it's lunch in a cocktail lounge where the spoons are chipped as a
black habit, you insect.

This is screeched as fuck.
Ushers the ripe into rooms calling Madrid.
Fingers of statues homes, reader.

Pantopon dogs
humming glycerine heroin gentle
aftosa squirms, in reply.

It is colourless as emotion tied up and mangled Tangiers scars and bites, sucker.

Arrested halos over clothing and palms, chilli hustler.

Always the east wing of yes moving and glad,
died as seeds to spill into sewers of white burlesque need.

Tainted match dead. Light as grain. Tentative. Nods of heroin.
Maize rackets for Mayans. Speeches on fire.

It throws smooth brown
units over small faces.
Smells young. Overdoses in minutes.

This is sharp in the
husk of commerce. Purple as solids.
Heaps of diseased walkers heaving.

A twisted area of yen.
Exposed pipe presence.
Naked photos of putty birds
decorate two-dimensional
libidos.

A flash
of twinge and tell cunts.

Queer needles stir traps heavy with galoshes
on the knees of adolescence.
Lonesome as silver. Easing pain of muttering
kidneys while rumblers on the side
silently copulate with rubber orifices.

A squawking orgasm
hanging in fields of screams
dank as carbide in 1920.
A good seat depresses the
hypothalamus of rusty table hammers.
Deadens scattered seas of jisom
numb and tumescent pink.

Burning and
toothless convoluted. Reeks
of dark plains and sky nerves.
Holding pants first with
heat silent syringes in hand,
ten gasoline mouths gumming flesh.

It is hairless, chum. Junk walks and happens. Fades. Testicles month pounded and kicked. Cures fall atrophied and ectoplasmic. Broken material touched by thirty lost lanterns.

Skulls over rotting bones. Consumed motion vibrating slow to smudge open cans white and cold.

On film at noon fires carry flesh junkies enveloped in grey, waiting to taste.

Montparnasse is a smeared mouth, a phantom scavenger of words, a mendicant of soft.

SOME NOTES ON PLUNDER
& INFLUENCES

Alice is a series of journal entries, which come from my imagination and researching all the sources listed. While the characters are based on historical figures, I've extrapolated and reimagined them to suit my own purposes.

Mirrors are embedded in the Alice section and use vocabulary from *The Mirror: a History* and is inspired by surrealism, the paintings of Salvador Dalí, and Max Ernst in particular.

Tales of Montparnasse is a mash up of various texts, including *Kiki's Memoirs, A Moveable Feast, Memoirs of Montparnasse* and *The Secret Paris of the 30s.* They say that Tzara inspired the cut up movement at a surrealist rally in the 20s when he offered to create a poem by pulling words at random out of a hat. Rather than a hat, I used a big box.

Opium takes its vocabulary from an amalgam of the *Secret Paris of the 30s*, *Vocabulaire Plain-Chant, Opium, the Diary of a Cure* and my own descriptions of the films *Blood of a Poet* and *Orpheus* from the Orpheus trilogy with a dash of Coleridge's *Kubla Khan* thrown in. The epigraph to this section is from *Opium, the Diary of a Cure*.

In which K meets B in a dream is an edited cut up from *Naked Lunch* with my own dreamt up additions.

SOURCES

Ballet mécanique. Dir. Fernand ger. Synchro-ciné [production company], 1924.

Bocquet, José-Louis. *Kiki de Montparnasse.* Trans. Nora Mahony. London: SelfMadeHero, 2011.

Bonnet, Sabine. *The mirror: a history.* Trans. Katherine H. Jewett. New York: Routledge, 2001.

Brassaï, *The secret Paris of the 30's.* New York: Pantheon Books, 1976.

Breton, André. *Conversations: The Autobiography of Surrealism.* Trans. Mark Polizzotti. New York: Paragon House, 1993.

Burroughs, William S. *Naked Lunch: the restored text.* Eds. James Grauerholz and Barry Miles. New York: Grove Press, 2001.

Callaghan, Morley. *That summer in Paris.* Toronto: Exile Editions, 2006.

Charters, Jimmie, and Morrill Cody. *This must be the place: memoirs of Montparnasse.* Ed. Hugo Ford. New York: Collier Books, 1989.

Christy, Jim. *Scalawags-Rogues, Roustabouts, Wags & Scamps— Brazen Ne'er-Do-Wells Through the Ages.* Vancouver, BC.: Anvil Press, 2008.

Cocteau, Jean. *Opium; the diary of a cure.* Trans. Margaret Crossland and Sinclair Road. London: Peter Owen Ltd, 1957.

Cocteau, Jean. *Vocabulaire; Plain-chant; L'ange heurtebise; Par lui-même; Cherchez Apollon; L'incendie; Léone; La crucifixion.* Paris: Gallimard, 1983.

Glassco, John. *Memoirs of Montparnasse.* New York: the New York Review of Books, 2007.

Hemingway, Ernest, *A moveable feast New York.* Scribner, 1992.

Klüver; Billy, and Julie Martin.. Eds. *Kiki's memoirs.* Hopewell, N.J.: The Ecco Press, 1996.

Klüver; Billy, and Julie Martin. *Kiki's Paris: artists and lovers 1900–1930.* New York: Abrams, 1989.

Le sang d'un poete. Dir. Jean Cocteau. Criterion Collection, 2000.

Lottman, Herbert R.. *Man Ray's Montparnasse.* New York: H.N. Abrams, 2001.

Man Ray. *Self portrait.* 1st ed. Boston: Little, Brown, 1963.

McAlmon, Robert. *Being geniuses together, 1920–1930.* London: The Hogarth Press, 1984.

Orphée. Dir. Jean Cocteau. Hollywood Film Exchange, 1971949.

Stein, Gertrude. *The autobiography of Alice B. Toklas.* New York: Vintage Books, 1961.

Wiser, William. *The Twilight Years, Paris in the 1930s.* New York. Carroll and Graf, 2000.

ACKNOWLEDGEMENTS

I am grateful to the City of Ottawa and the Ontario Arts Council for their funding.

Thanks to dear friends Emily Falvey, Christine McNair, Roland Prevost, Sean Moreland, Warren Dean Fulton, Monty Reid, John Lavery, Marcus McCann, and Pearl Pirie for ongoing interest and encouragement, and to Steven Heighton for his initial read and encouragement. To rob mclennan for teaching me it's ok to play. And a special thank you to my first reader and dear friend, Sandra Ridley.

Thank you to Ren Tomovcik for the gift of José-Louis Bocquet's *Kiki de Montparnasse*.

Tremendous gratitude to Ottawa's many reading series which make it possible for a neophyte poetess to try out her work on unsuspecting and tolerant audiences.

Some of these poems have appeared in *Kiki* (excerpts), Laurel Reed Books, 2010. Thanks to Kemeny Babineau for publishing the teaser.

I made a spin off chapbook as part of Dan Waber's this is visual poetry series based on the personae of Montparnasse. Thanks to Dan Waber.

With love and thanks to my husband, Charles, for his love, support, inspiration and photography.

Writers of epics are no more concerned about wigs and wrong dates than Homer with geography and metamorphoses.

Jean Cocteau, *Opium– the Diary of a Cure*

This otherness, this
"Not-being-us" is all there is to look at
In the mirror,

John Ashbery, *Self Portrait in a Convex Mirror*

Dedicated to those who came after

David Lynch, Gwendolyn MacEwen, Alan Moore

Nan Goldin, Jean-Michel Basquiat, Bob Dylan

bpNichol, Douglas Coupland, Iggy Pop

Glenn Gould, Lou Reed, bill bissett

Nathanaël, Andy Warhol, Leslie Scalapino

jwcurry, Ubu Web, Jon Paul Fiorentino

Influency Salon, Gary Barwin, Tim Burton

Julian Schnabel, Todd Haynes, Margaret Christakos

Tom Waits, David Byrne

Lisa Robertson, David Bowie, Angela Rawlings

Anne Carson, Christian Bök, Erín Moure

John Lennon, derek beaulieu, Philip Glass

Glenn Nuotio, Book Thug, the a b series

Oliver Schröer

Paul Quarrington

Mark Rothko

BIOGRAPHY

Amanda Earl is a poet, publisher and pornographer from Ottawa, Ontario, Canada. Amanda's most recent chapbooks are the 2012 chapbook *Sex First & Then A Sandwich* (her third chapbook with above/ground press) and *Me, Medusa* (Red Ceilings Press, UK, 2012). Her poetry appears in magazines such as *Rampike, the White Wall Review, fillingStation,* in addition to online and print journals in Australia, Canada, England, France, Ireland and the USA. Over the course of her research for this book, she has become fascinated with Montparnasse between the wars and is an avid appreciator of books, films, art and music from the era. More information can be found at KikiFolle.com.

Library and Archives Canada Cataloguing in Publication

Earl, Amanda Charlotte, author
    Kiki / Amanda Earl.

Poems.
ISBN 978-0-9783428-9-0 (pbk.)

    I. Title.

PS8559.A3194K53 2014   C811'.6   C2014-905538-2

COLOPHON

Typeset in Garamond Premier Pro by Christine McNair and printed at Marquis Printing. Garamond Premier Pro was originally conceived by Adobe designer Robert Slimbach in 1988. The typeface re-interprets the metal punches and type designs of Claude Garamond produced in the mid 1500s.

www.chaudierebooks.com